BIG BOOK OF BUGS

Theresa Greenaway

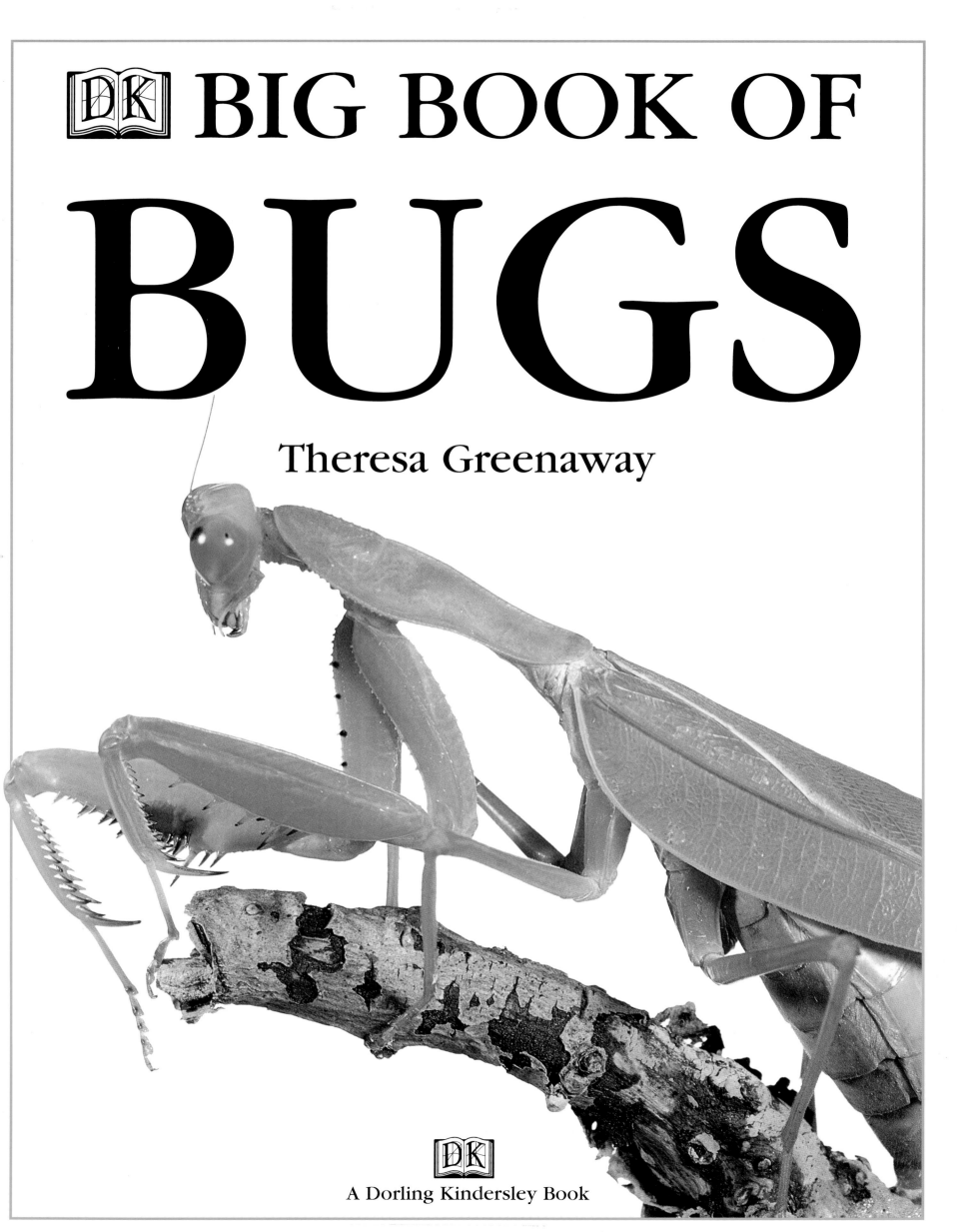

A Dorling Kindersley Book

Dorling **DK** Kindersley

LONDON, NEW YORK, SYDNEY, DELHI, PARIS,
MUNICH, and JOHANNESBURG

Senior Editor Shaila Awan
Senior Art Editor Mandy Earey
Designer Jane Buckley

Publishing Manager Sarah Phillips
Deputy Art Director Mark Richards
DTP Designer Megan Clayton
Jacket Designer Giles Powell-Smith
Picture Researcher Angela Anderson
Production Melanie Dowland
Photography Jane Burton, Geoff Dann,
Neil Fletcher, Frank Greenaway,
Colin Keates, Harry Taylor, Kim Taylor

First American Edition, 2000

10

013-KG249-Sep/00

Published in the United States by
Dorling Kindersley Publishing, Inc.
375 Hudson Street New York, New York 10014

Library of Congress Cataloging-in-Publication Data

Greenaway, Theresa, 1947-
DK big book of bugs / by Theresa Greenaway.- - 1st American ed.
  p. cm.
Summary: Text and detailed photographs offer facts about a
wide variety of insects, including beetles, wasps, and stick
and leaf insects.
ISBN-13: 978-0-7894-6520-7
I. Insects - - Juvenile literature. (1. Insects.) I. Title: Big book
of bugs. II. Title: Bugs. III. DK Publishing, Inc. IV. Title
QL467.2.G737 2000
                                                           00-023899

Color reproduction by Classicscan, Singapore
Printed in China by South China Printing Co. Ltd

The publisher would like to thank the following for their
kind permission to reproduce their photographs:
a=above, b=bottom, c=center, t=top, l=left, r=right

Bruce Coleman Ltd: Alain Compost 13tl; M. P. L. Fogden 29tr;
John Shaw 10-11; Jan Taylor 16cl; Kim Taylor 7cr, 10cl, 23br;
Kina Nature Library: 14r; **Natural History Museum:** 26cr;
N.H.P.A.: Anthony Bannister 25tr; G. J. Cambridge 5crb;
Stephen Dalton 10-11, 19tr, 29tl; John Shaw 22-23;
Planet Earth Pictures: Geoff du Feu 11tr; Peter Gasson 31cr;
David P. Maitland 12cl; **Premaphotos Wildlife:** 21tl;
K G Preston-Mafham 24b, 27tr, 26cr, 28cl.

See our complete
catalog at
www.dk.com

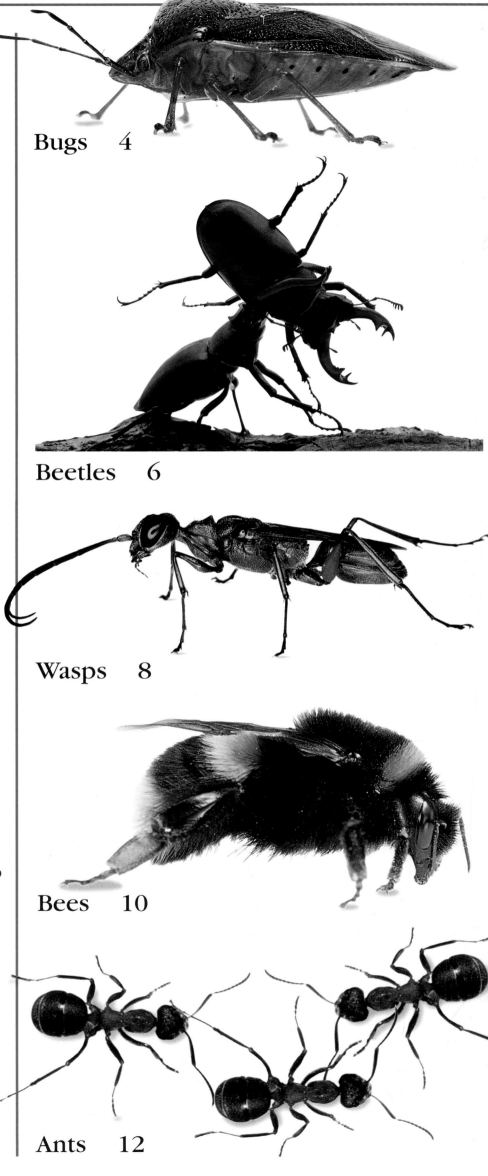

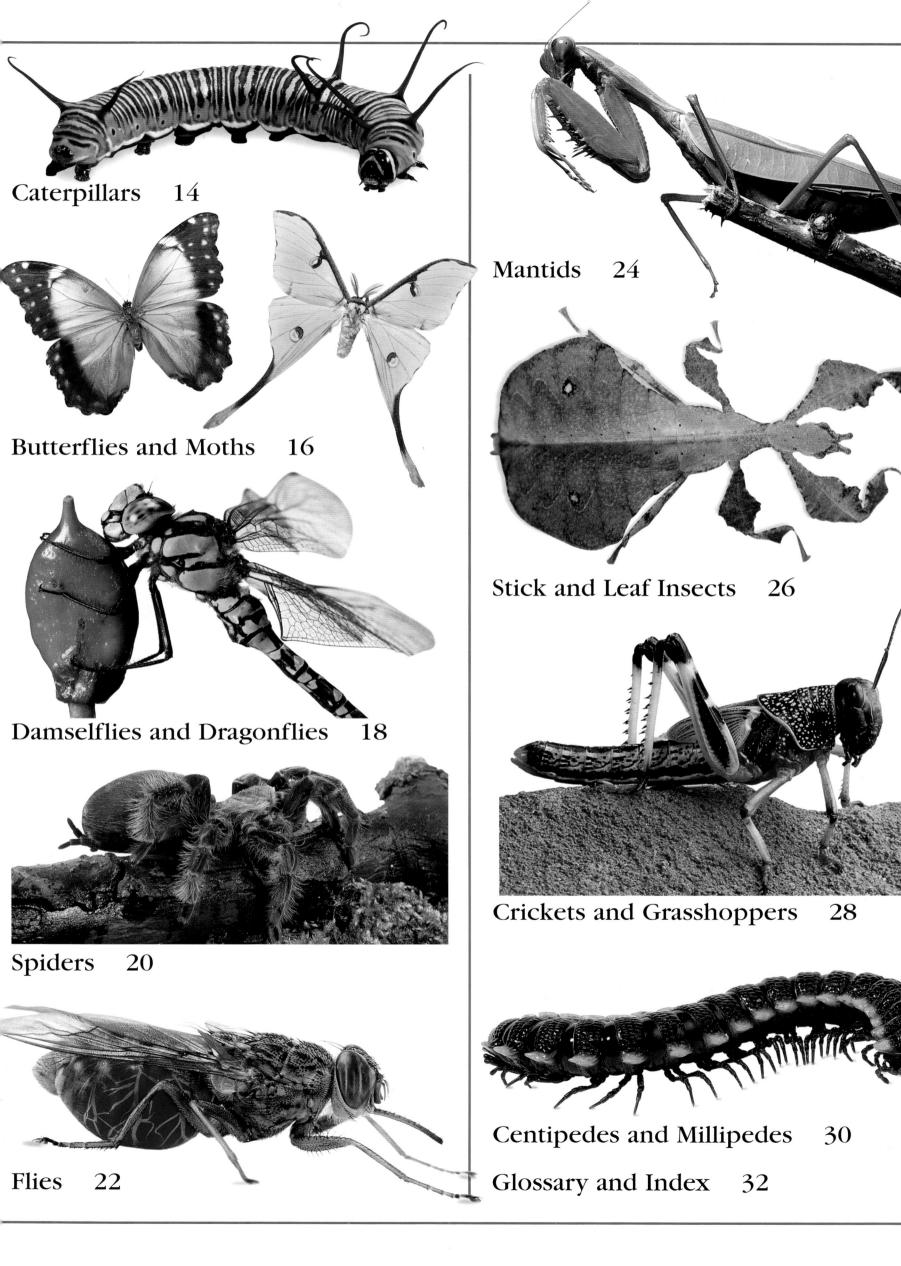

Bugs

Some people call all insects bugs, but true bugs are a particular group of insects with special mouthparts that can pierce and suck. Many of these bugs pierce the stems and leaves of plants to suck the sweet sap. Some hunt insects. Others, such as bedbugs, pierce the skin of sleeping humans to suck their blood!

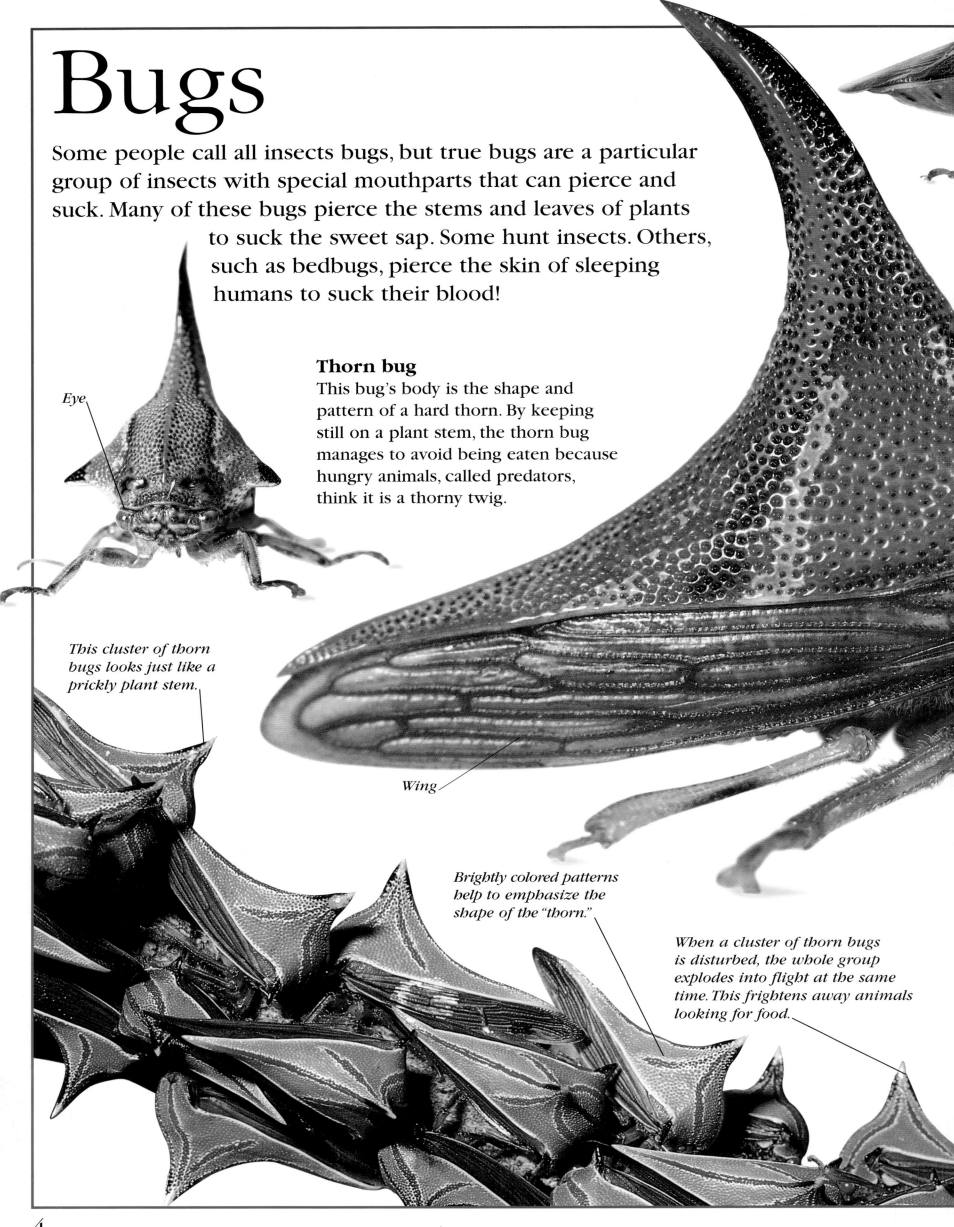

Eye

Thorn bug
This bug's body is the shape and pattern of a hard thorn. By keeping still on a plant stem, the thorn bug manages to avoid being eaten because hungry animals, called predators, think it is a thorny twig.

This cluster of thorn bugs looks just like a prickly plant stem.

Wing

Brightly colored patterns help to emphasize the shape of the "thorn."

When a cluster of thorn bugs is disturbed, the whole group explodes into flight at the same time. This frightens away animals looking for food.

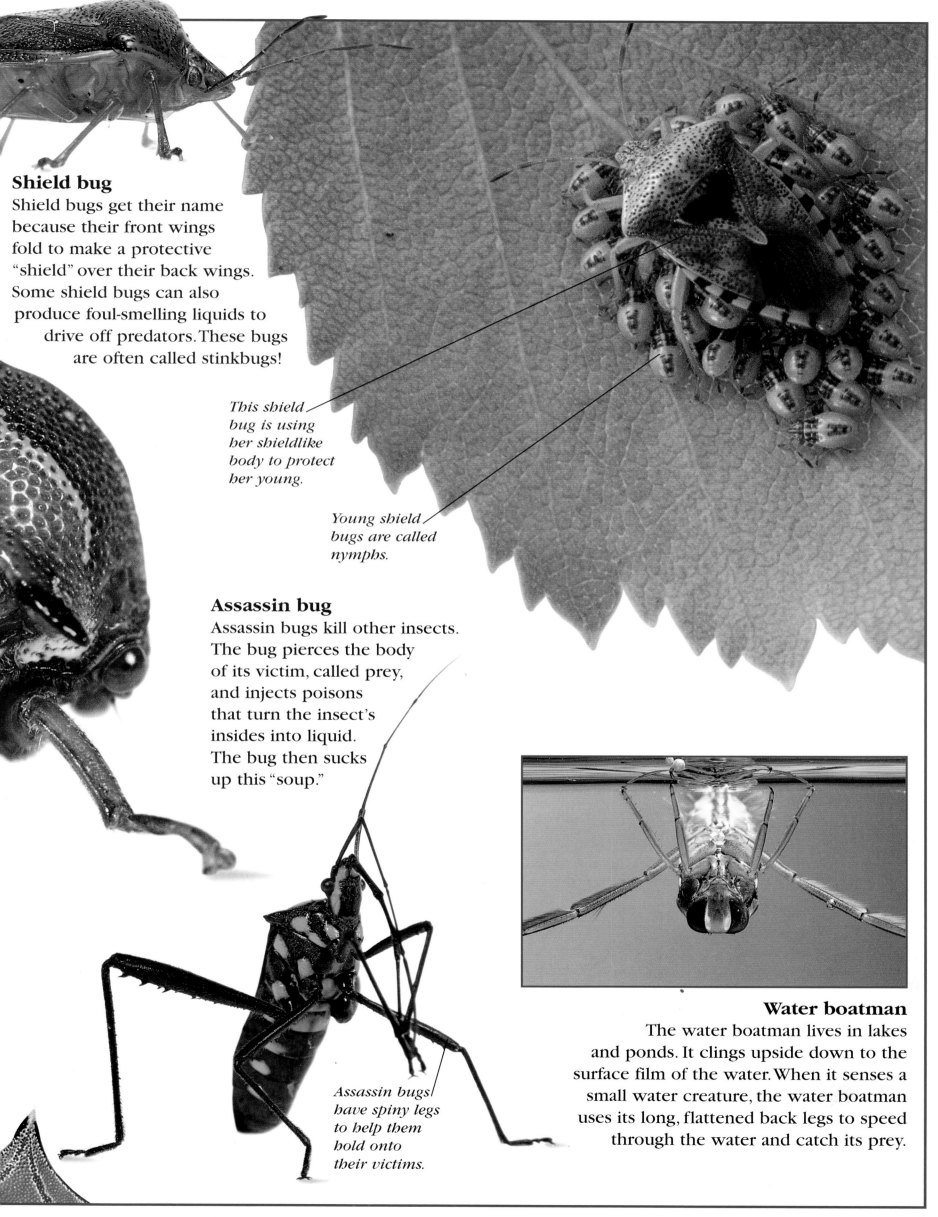

Shield bug

Shield bugs get their name because their front wings fold to make a protective "shield" over their back wings. Some shield bugs can also produce foul-smelling liquids to drive off predators. These bugs are often called stinkbugs!

This shield bug is using her shieldlike body to protect her young.

Young shield bugs are called nymphs.

Assassin bug

Assassin bugs kill other insects. The bug pierces the body of its victim, called prey, and injects poisons that turn the insect's insides into liquid. The bug then sucks up this "soup."

Assassin bugs have spiny legs to help them hold onto their victims.

Water boatman

The water boatman lives in lakes and ponds. It clings upside down to the surface film of the water. When it senses a small water creature, the water boatman uses its long, flattened back legs to speed through the water and catch its prey.

Beetles

There are more than 300,000 different kinds of beetle. This makes beetles the largest group of animals in the world! Beetles live in many different places, from tropical rain forests and scorching deserts to snowy mountains and garden ponds.

Stag beetles
Male stag beetles have large, antlerlike jaws that give them their name. They use them in wrestling matches with each other when they fight for female stag beetles.

Fighting males try to pick each other up in their jaws. The winner is the beetle that overturns his opponent. The beetles often hurt each other in these fights.

Hooks, spines, and hairs on all six legs help the beetle cling to fruit and twigs.

The hard front wing cases help to protect the thin wings that are folded underneath.

Goliath beetle
The Goliath beetle is the heaviest beetle in the world. It weighs as much as an apple and is as big as your hand! Goliath beetles live in the treetops of tropical rain forests in Africa, where they feed on fruit.

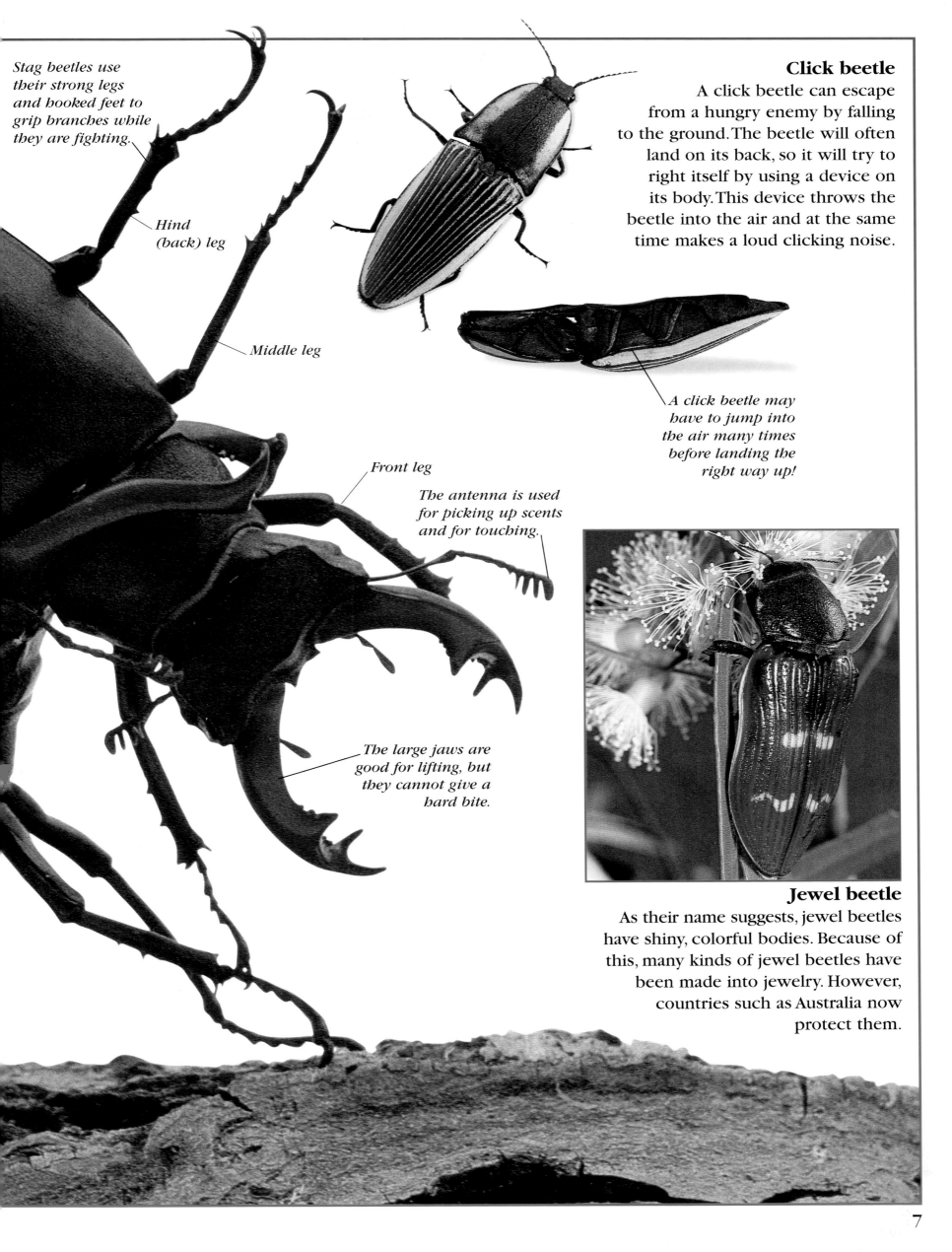

Stag beetles use their strong legs and hooked feet to grip branches while they are fighting.

Hind (back) leg

Middle leg

Front leg

The antenna is used for picking up scents and for touching.

The large jaws are good for lifting, but they cannot give a hard bite.

Click beetle

A click beetle can escape from a hungry enemy by falling to the ground. The beetle will often land on its back, so it will try to right itself by using a device on its body. This device throws the beetle into the air and at the same time makes a loud clicking noise.

A click beetle may have to jump into the air many times before landing the right way up!

Jewel beetle

As their name suggests, jewel beetles have shiny, colorful bodies. Because of this, many kinds of jewel beetles have been made into jewelry. However, countries such as Australia now protect them.

Wasps

Wasps frighten people because many of these insects have powerful stingers, but painful encounters between wasps and people are accidental. Wasps do use their stingers when they feel threatened by us, but their stingers' main use is to inject poison that helps to paralyze or kill their prey.

Ichneumon wasp

Female ichneumon wasps have long egg-laying tubes. They use these to insert their eggs inside another insect, such as a caterpillar.

Jewel wasp

This jewel wasp lives in the tropical rain forests of Asia, where she hunts for crickets and grasshoppers. She uses her stinger to paralyze her victim and then drags it to a burrow. When the wasp egg hatches, the grub feeds on the insect.

The wasp's beautiful green color shines like a jewel.

German wasp

This wasp has strong jaws, which she uses to chop up food and to help build her papery nest. A German wasp may live in a colony of up to two thousand wasps. Animals learn quickly that these yellow-and-black wasps give very painful stings!

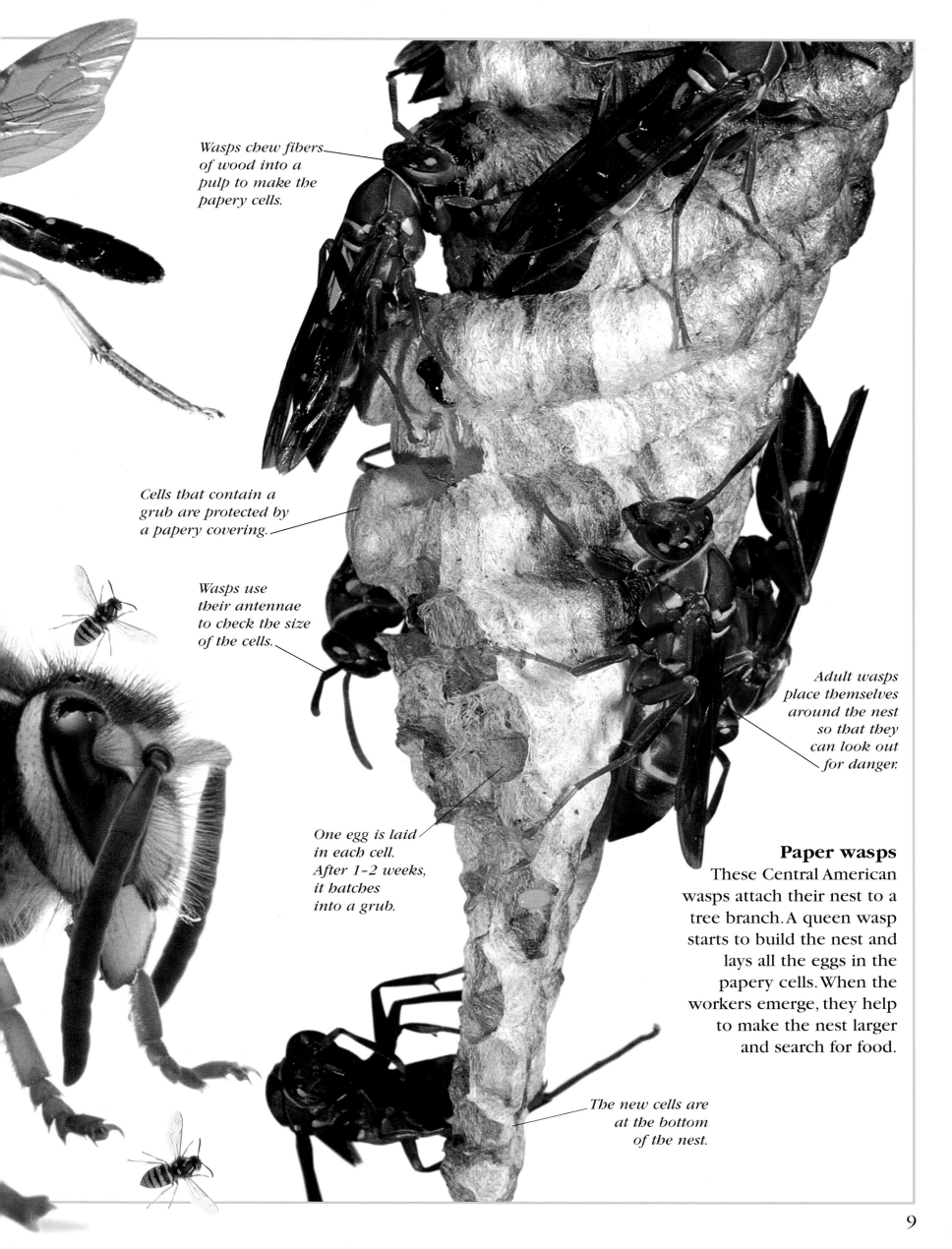

Wasps chew fibers of wood into a pulp to make the papery cells.

Cells that contain a grub are protected by a papery covering.

Wasps use their antennae to check the size of the cells.

One egg is laid in each cell. After 1-2 weeks, it hatches into a grub.

Adult wasps place themselves around the nest so that they can look out for danger.

Paper wasps
These Central American wasps attach their nest to a tree branch. A queen wasp starts to build the nest and lays all the eggs in the papery cells. When the workers emerge, they help to make the nest larger and search for food.

The new cells are at the bottom of the nest.

9

Bees

Honeybees and bumblebees live in groups called colonies. In each colony there are lots of worker bees, but only one egg-laying queen bee. Worker bees gather food and look after the young bee grubs. Solitary bees, such as leafcutter bees, live by themselves. They make small nests with a few cells.

Worker honeybees

A worker honeybee visits flowers to collect nectar and pollen, which she carries back to the hive. The nectar (a sweet liquid) is used to make honey, which is stored inside the hive. Honey is eaten by the adult bees, while the bee grubs are fed both honey and pollen.

This worker honeybee will fly back to the hive to tell the other workers where she has found lots of sweet nectar.

Pollen clings to hairs on the bee's shiny body and legs.

This queen honeybee lays all the eggs needed for the hive. She is cared for by the worker honeybees, which are all females.

Leafcutter bee

This bee snips neat pieces of leaf to line its cell made in a hollow stem or a small hole. A leafcutter bee will even use the keyhole in a shed door! The female then fills the cell with pollen and lays her egg.

A bee's stinger is hidden inside the tip of its abdomen.

A bumblebee has a furry body and furry legs. This helps it to keep warm when the weather is cold.

Bumblebee

A queen bumblebee often uses an old vole burrow for her nest. Her workers gather food and tend the grubs just like honeybees, but they do not make honey. In the fall, all bumblebees die except for the new young queens. These hibernate (sleep) until spring.

Ants

Most kinds of ants live in huge colonies. Thousands of worker ants build a nest to house the colony. They care for the queen ant and the young. The workers also leave the nest to search for food. Many ants are fierce hunters.

Bulldog ant

It is not a good idea to get too close to the nest made by bulldog ants! They have good eyesight, and as soon as they see anything approaching, they run and leap to the attack. Each ant has a pair of sharp, spiny jaws that can give a painful bite. A bulldog ant can also sting. This is as painful as a wasp's sting!

Leafcutter ants

Leafcutter ants snip pieces from leaves and flowers. Then they carry them back to their nest. Here, other workers act as gardeners by cutting up the leaf pieces and using them to grow fungus, which the ants use for food.

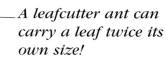

A leafcutter ant can carry a leaf twice its own size!

These ants are often called "parasol" ants because of the way each ant carries its piece of leaf. ("Parasol" is another word for "umbrella.")

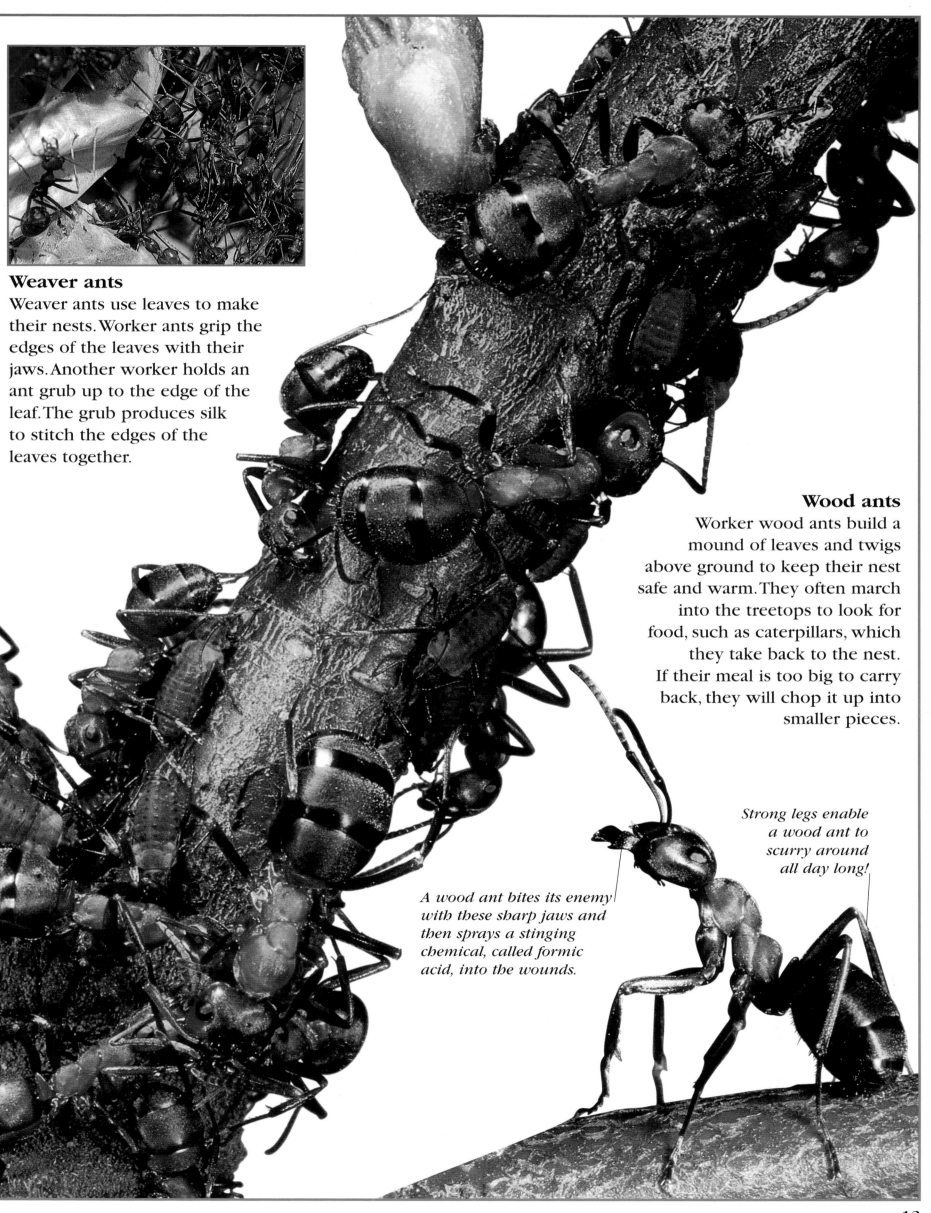

Weaver ants

Weaver ants use leaves to make their nests. Worker ants grip the edges of the leaves with their jaws. Another worker holds an ant grub up to the edge of the leaf. The grub produces silk to stitch the edges of the leaves together.

Wood ants

Worker wood ants build a mound of leaves and twigs above ground to keep their nest safe and warm. They often march into the treetops to look for food, such as caterpillars, which they take back to the nest. If their meal is too big to carry back, they will chop it up into smaller pieces.

Strong legs enable a wood ant to scurry around all day long!

A wood ant bites its enemy with these sharp jaws and then sprays a stinging chemical, called formic acid, into the wounds.

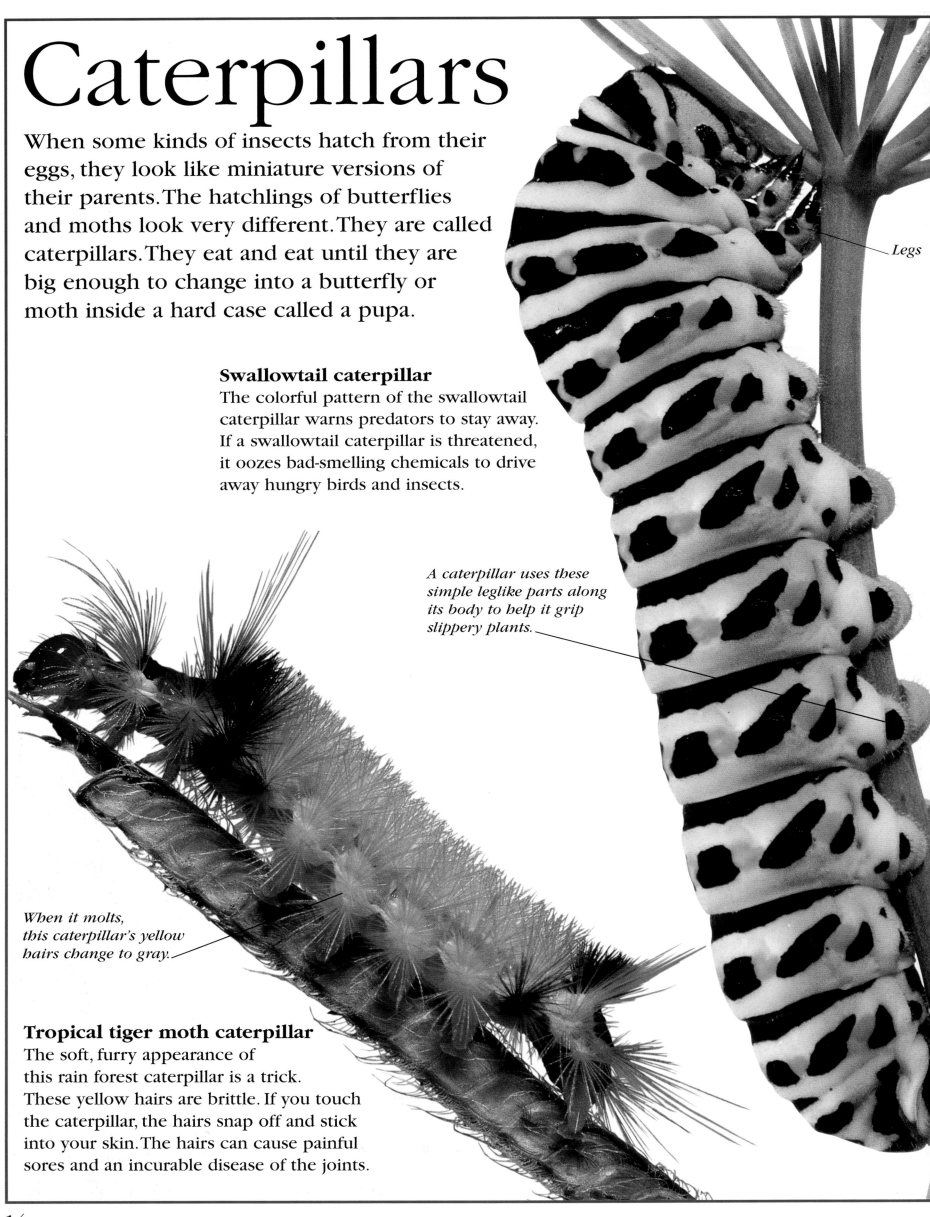

Caterpillars

When some kinds of insects hatch from their eggs, they look like miniature versions of their parents. The hatchlings of butterflies and moths look very different. They are called caterpillars. They eat and eat until they are big enough to change into a butterfly or moth inside a hard case called a pupa.

Legs

Swallowtail caterpillar
The colorful pattern of the swallowtail caterpillar warns predators to stay away. If a swallowtail caterpillar is threatened, it oozes bad-smelling chemicals to drive away hungry birds and insects.

A caterpillar uses these simple leglike parts along its body to help it grip slippery plants.

When it molts, this caterpillar's yellow hairs change to gray.

Tropical tiger moth caterpillar
The soft, furry appearance of this rain forest caterpillar is a trick. These yellow hairs are brittle. If you touch the caterpillar, the hairs snap off and stick into your skin. The hairs can cause painful sores and an incurable disease of the joints.

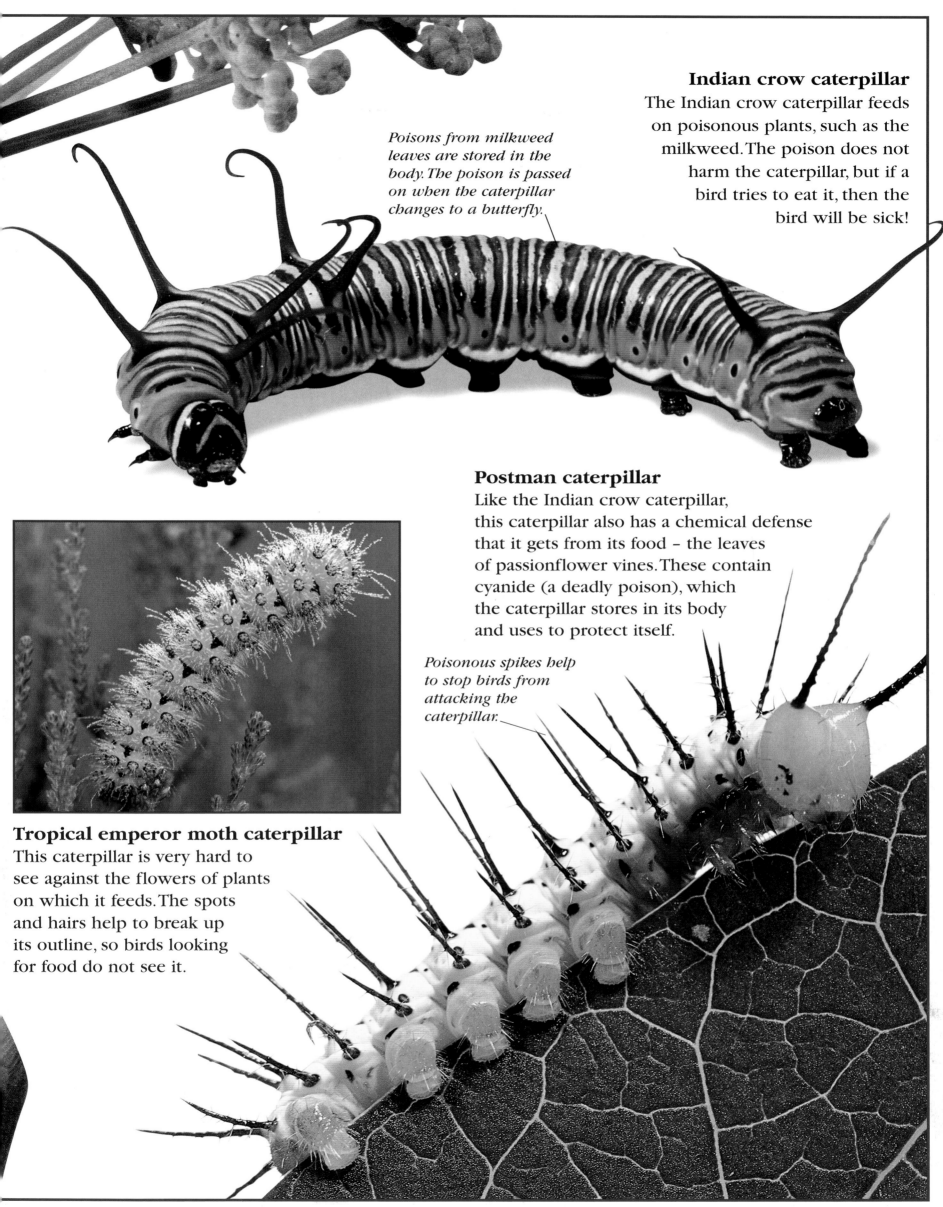

Indian crow caterpillar

The Indian crow caterpillar feeds on poisonous plants, such as the milkweed. The poison does not harm the caterpillar, but if a bird tries to eat it, then the bird will be sick!

Poisons from milkweed leaves are stored in the body. The poison is passed on when the caterpillar changes to a butterfly.

Postman caterpillar

Like the Indian crow caterpillar, this caterpillar also has a chemical defense that it gets from its food – the leaves of passionflower vines. These contain cyanide (a deadly poison), which the caterpillar stores in its body and uses to protect itself.

Poisonous spikes help to stop birds from attacking the caterpillar.

Tropical emperor moth caterpillar

This caterpillar is very hard to see against the flowers of plants on which it feeds. The spots and hairs help to break up its outline, so birds looking for food do not see it.

Butterflies and Moths

Each butterfly and moth has two pairs of wings covered with tiny scales that overlap like tiles on a roof. These scales give butterfly and moth wings their beautiful colors and patterns. Unlike the leaf-eating caterpillars, these insects feed on nectar.

Blue morpho butterfly

The shiny blue color of morpho butterflies is so brilliant that they have been made into jewelry. This amazing color can only be seen when the wings are open. On the underside, the wings are brown.

Monarch butterfly

In the fall, thousands of monarch butterflies from the eastern US and Canada fly south to California and Mexico, where the weather is warmer. In the spring, they start the long journey home.

The brightly colored wings warn birds that this butterfly tastes bad.

A butterfly uses its mouth tube like a drinking straw to sip nectar.

Postman butterfly

A female postman butterfly lays her eggs on the tips of young passionflower shoots. She only chooses plants that have no eggs on them so that the young caterpillars have plenty to eat.

African moon moth
The eyespots on the wings of this African moth confuse enemies or trick them into thinking the wings are part of a large, scary head. The "tails" on the hind wings snap off if the moth is pecked. This too helps to prevent the moth's body from attack.

Eyespots on all four wings make an animal feel that it is being watched.

Cinnabar moth
A cinnabar moth flies by day as well as by night. It has a slow, fluttery flight, but it is safe from predators – the red color warns birds that it is very poisonous.

The wings fold over the moth's body when it is resting.

Emperor moth
This moth lives in meadows and moorlands. The female emperor moth only flies at night. During the day, she relies on large eyespots on her wings to trick birds into thinking that an animal is watching them.

Damselflies and Dragonflies

Damselflies and dragonflies and their young, called nymphs, are fierce predators. Nymphs live and feed in water. The adults catch other insects in flight by using their sharp, spiny legs, which they hold out to make a kind of trap. Their huge eyes can detect the slightest movement that may mean food or danger.

Plants growing beside water give shelter from poor weather and enemies.

Each compound eye is made up of thousands of little lenses.

Beautiful demoiselle

The beautiful demoiselle lives over clear, fast-running streams. Like all damselflies, its wings are folded together above its back when it is resting. The damselfly has good eyesight, which helps it to hunt for food and keep a lookout for danger.

Because of their long, thin bodies, damselflies were once called "Devil's darning needles."

The long body is made up of many parts that enable the damselfly to bend.

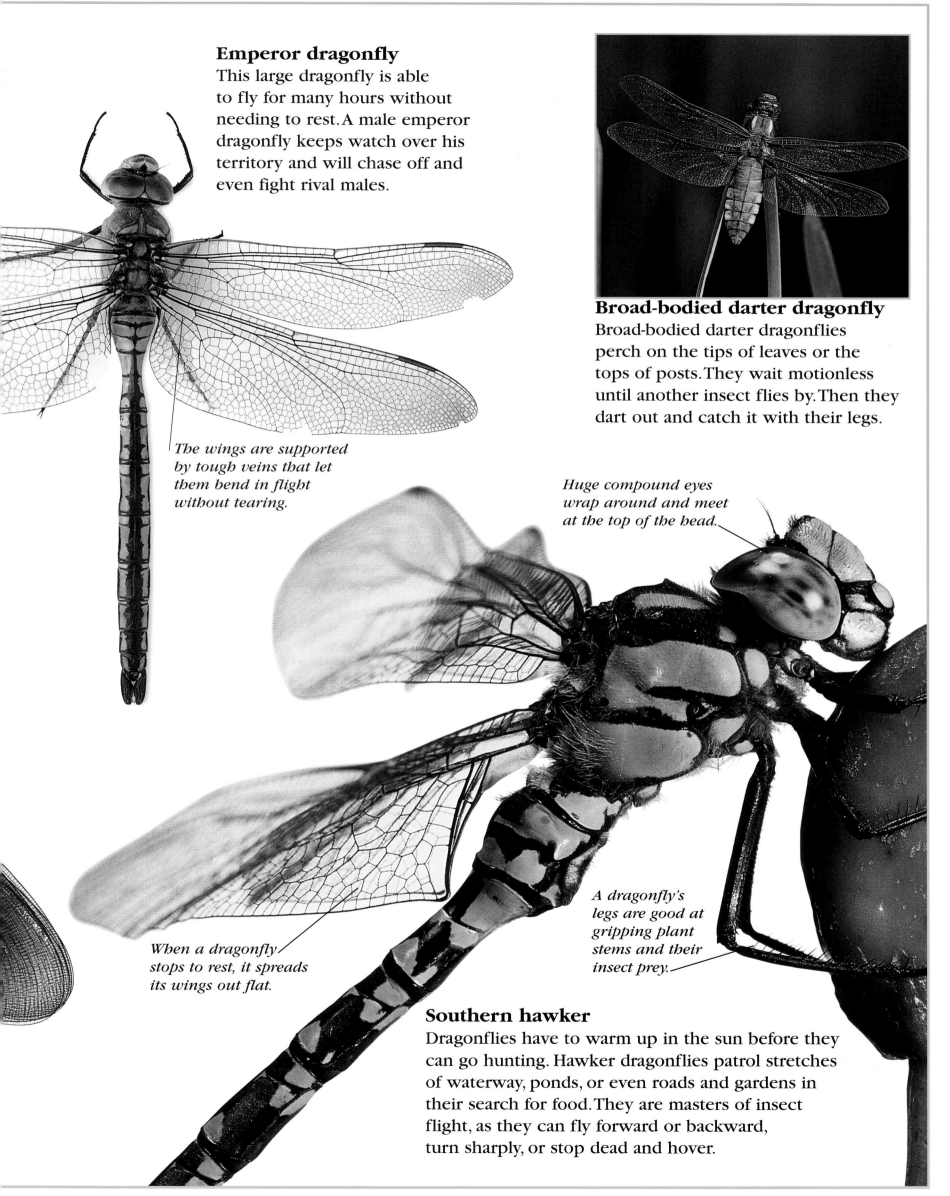

Emperor dragonfly

This large dragonfly is able to fly for many hours without needing to rest. A male emperor dragonfly keeps watch over his territory and will chase off and even fight rival males.

The wings are supported by tough veins that let them bend in flight without tearing.

Broad-bodied darter dragonfly

Broad-bodied darter dragonflies perch on the tips of leaves or the tops of posts. They wait motionless until another insect flies by. Then they dart out and catch it with their legs.

Huge compound eyes wrap around and meet at the top of the head.

When a dragonfly stops to rest, it spreads its wings out flat.

A dragonfly's legs are good at gripping plant stems and their insect prey.

Southern hawker

Dragonflies have to warm up in the sun before they can go hunting. Hawker dragonflies patrol stretches of waterway, ponds, or even roads and gardens in their search for food. They are masters of insect flight, as they can fly forward or backward, turn sharply, or stop dead and hover.

Spiders

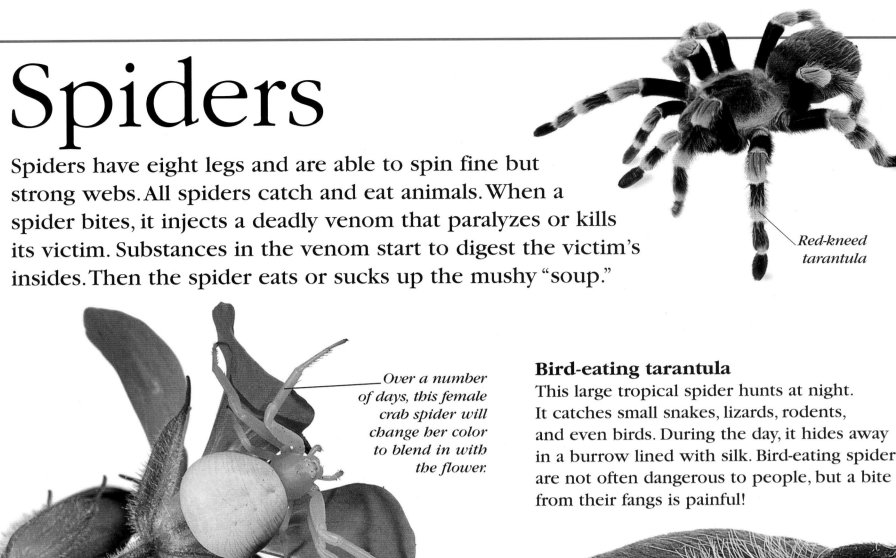

Spiders have eight legs and are able to spin fine but strong webs. All spiders catch and eat animals. When a spider bites, it injects a deadly venom that paralyzes or kills its victim. Substances in the venom start to digest the victim's insides. Then the spider eats or sucks up the mushy "soup."

Red-kneed tarantula

Over a number of days, this female crab spider will change her color to blend in with the flower.

Bird-eating tarantula

This large tropical spider hunts at night. It catches small snakes, lizards, rodents, and even birds. During the day, it hides away in a burrow lined with silk. Bird-eating spiders are not often dangerous to people, but a bite from their fangs is painful!

Crab spider

Female crab spiders hide among the petals of flowers. They can even change their color to match the flower. This helps crab spiders to ambush nectar-collecting insects without being spotted.

Orb spider

The orb spider uses silk to catch its prey. When an insect flies into the web, the spider runs across and bites it. Then the orb spider wraps the insect in sheets of silk to prevent it from struggling free before the poison takes effect.

Spokes of the web are spun first. Then the spider makes spiral threads.

Wolf spider

Wolf spiders are always on the hunt for food. A female wolf spider carries her spiderlings on her back even when she goes hunting. If a spiderling falls off, it climbs back up!

The spider flicks these long hairs at its enemies. The hairs stick into the skin and cause irritation.

Flies

Some flies are a nuisance to people and animals. They spread germs from dung onto food, while others carry diseases such as malaria. Not all flies are unpleasant, however. Hoverflies help to pollinate flowers, and some flies feed on harmful insects.

The fly pushes its thin mouthparts into the skin of animals.

After a good meal, the abdomen is swollen with blood.

Tsetse fly

The sharp mouthparts of tsetse flies pierce the skin of humans and animals to suck up blood. The flies also inject a tiny organism that causes sleeping sickness. This disease kills people and cattle in Africa, where the fly is found.

Like all flies, this robber fly only has one pair of wings. It folds them over its back while at rest or when feeding.

Crane fly

A crane fly has long wings, a long body, and very long, fragile legs. These legs snap off if anything grabs hold of them. Crane flies hide among damp vegetation during the day and become active at night. They fly slowly with their legs dangling down, which is why they are called daddy longlegs!

Houseflies

A housefly will feed on dung, meat, or even cake if it can't get any dung! It uses its mouthparts like a sponge for sucking up food. When it flies from dung or garbage on to your food, the housefly contaminates it with germs.

Robber fly

The large eyes of this fierce fly enable it to see other insects approaching. It catches its victim in midair. Then lands to feast on its victim by sucking it dry.

Flying insects are snatched from the air with these spiny legs.

Hoverfly

Gardeners are pleased to see plenty of hoverflies in summer. Adults feed on nectar and pollen from flowers, while each hoverfly grub eats hundreds of the greenflies that attack garden plants.

Although it is striped like a wasp, this hoverfly does not have a stinger.

Mantids

Mantids are patient predators. They sit and wait for their next meal to turn up. Anything small enough to catch is eaten. Mating can be a dangerous event for male mantids, especially because they are smaller than the females. If all goes well, the male survives to fly off to another female. If things go wrong, he may end up as the female's next meal!

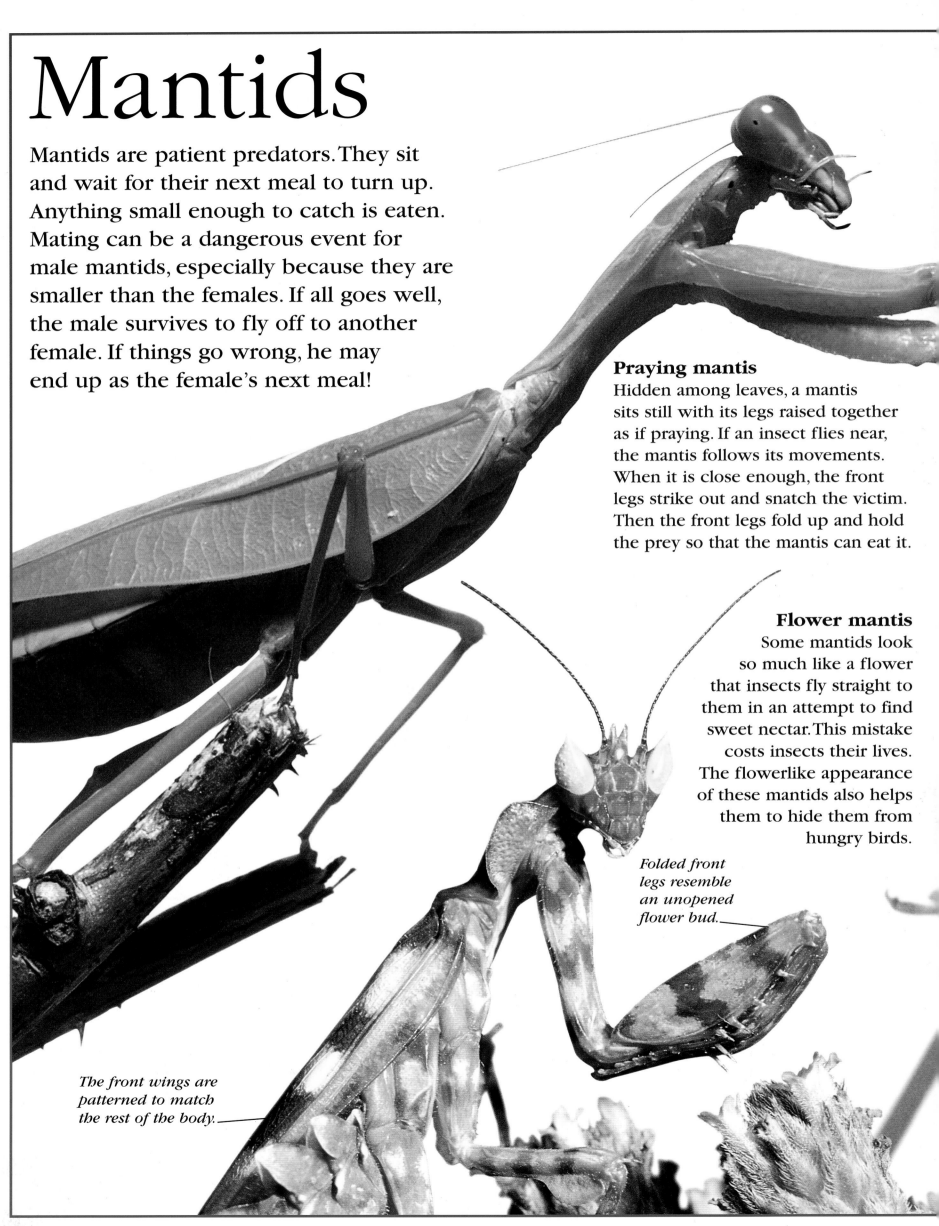

Praying mantis
Hidden among leaves, a mantis sits still with its legs raised together as if praying. If an insect flies near, the mantis follows its movements. When it is close enough, the front legs strike out and snatch the victim. Then the front legs fold up and hold the prey so that the mantis can eat it.

Flower mantis
Some mantids look so much like a flower that insects fly straight to them in an attempt to find sweet nectar. This mistake costs insects their lives. The flowerlike appearance of these mantids also helps them to hide them from hungry birds.

Folded front legs resemble an unopened flower bud.

The front wings are patterned to match the rest of the body.

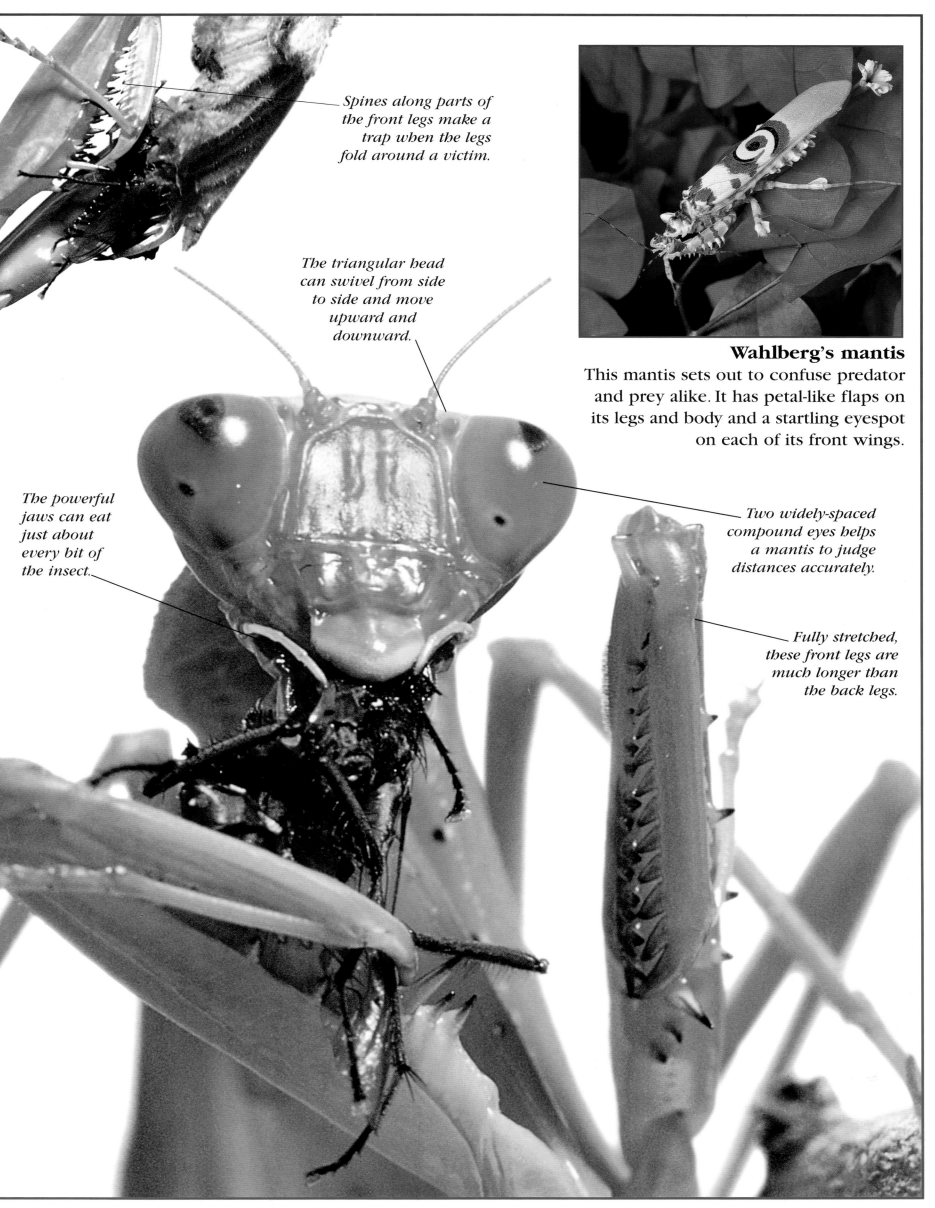

Spines along parts of
the front legs make a
trap when the legs
fold around a victim.

The triangular head
can swivel from side
to side and move
upward and
downward.

The powerful
jaws can eat
just about
every bit of
the insect.

Wahlberg's mantis
This mantis sets out to confuse predator
and prey alike. It has petal-like flaps on
its legs and body and a startling eyespot
on each of its front wings.

Two widely-spaced
compound eyes helps
a mantis to judge
distances accurately.

Fully stretched,
these front legs are
much longer than
the back legs.

Stick and Leaf Insects

Clever camouflage helps insects to stay alive in a world full of insect-eating animals. Stick and leaf insects avoid danger by hiding on thin stems, spiky twigs, or half-eaten leaves. They look so much like them that the stick and leaf insects are almost invisible! In the day, these insects stay still in one place. At night, they move around so that they can munch on leaves or find mates.

Malaysian stick insect
Stick insects not only look like twigs, they behave like them, too. They spend the day in the sort of place that a fallen twig would land on – stuck in the center of a large, curved leaf. When they have to move, they sway from side to side, like twigs quivering in a breeze.

When this stick insect is resting, the front legs are held out straight and the back legs are tucked along the sides of the body.

Giant stick insect
Most stick insects are wingless, but the Australian stick insect has colored wings. If it is threatened, the stick insect suddenly opens its wings and flashes them to try to scare away the predator.

There are many thorny or spiky plants in the forests where these stick insects live.

Eye

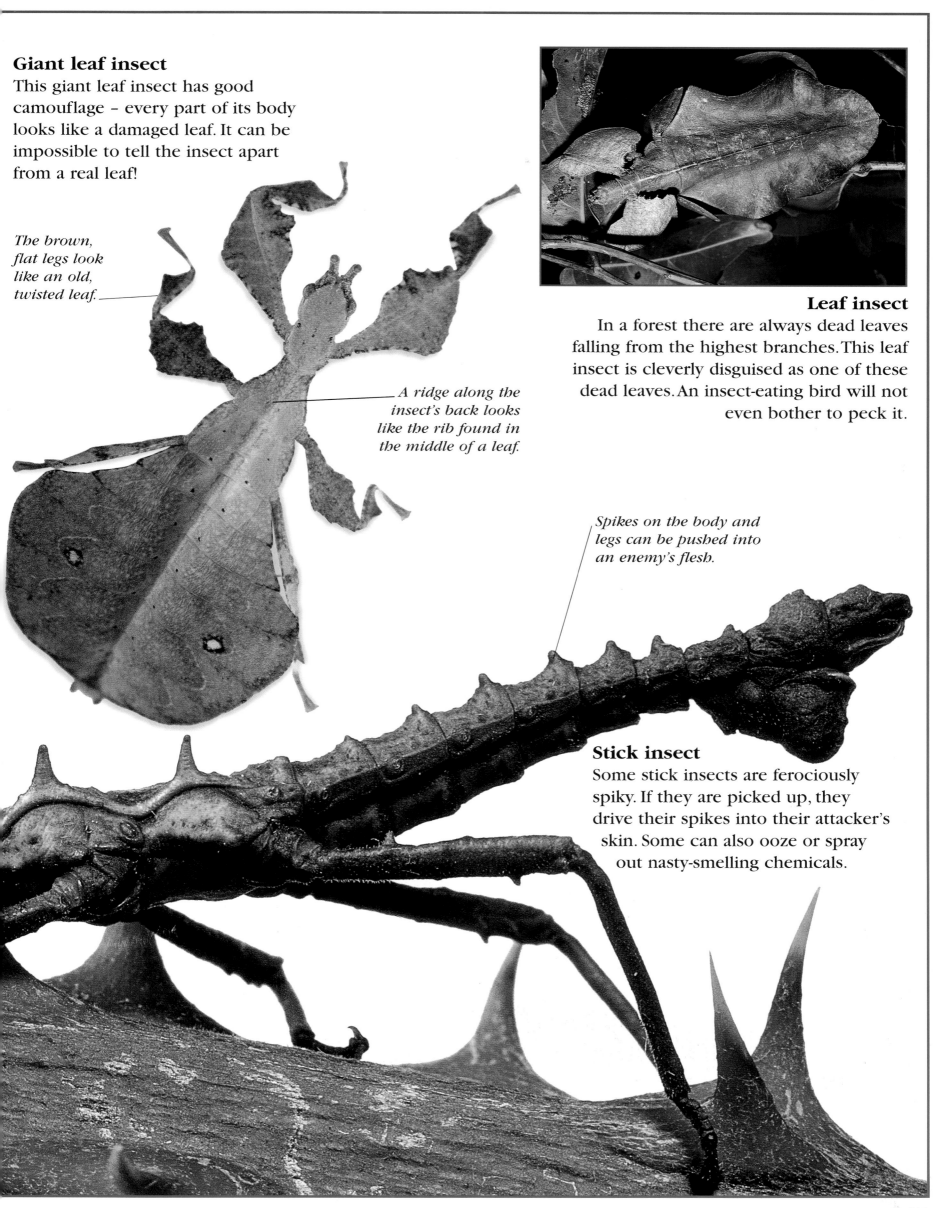

Giant leaf insect

This giant leaf insect has good camouflage – every part of its body looks like a damaged leaf. It can be impossible to tell the insect apart from a real leaf!

The brown, flat legs look like an old, twisted leaf.

A ridge along the insect's back looks like the rib found in the middle of a leaf.

Leaf insect

In a forest there are always dead leaves falling from the highest branches. This leaf insect is cleverly disguised as one of these dead leaves. An insect-eating bird will not even bother to peck it.

Spikes on the body and legs can be pushed into an enemy's flesh.

Stick insect

Some stick insects are ferociously spiky. If they are picked up, they drive their spikes into their attacker's skin. Some can also ooze or spray out nasty-smelling chemicals.

Crickets and Grasshoppers

Grasshoppers and crickets are often heard long before they are seen. Grasshoppers make their sounds by scraping their back legs against their wings. Most crickets scrape parts of their wings together to make their chirping songs. The sounds that they make help them to attract mates. But where are their ears? Grasshoppers have ears on their abdomen. Crickets have ears on their front legs!

Kenyan cricket
Most crickets hide. They rely on dull colors to avoid attracting attention. But this Kenyan cricket sits out in the open. Its blue pattern sends out a message that it is not good to eat!

A young locust is called a hopper.

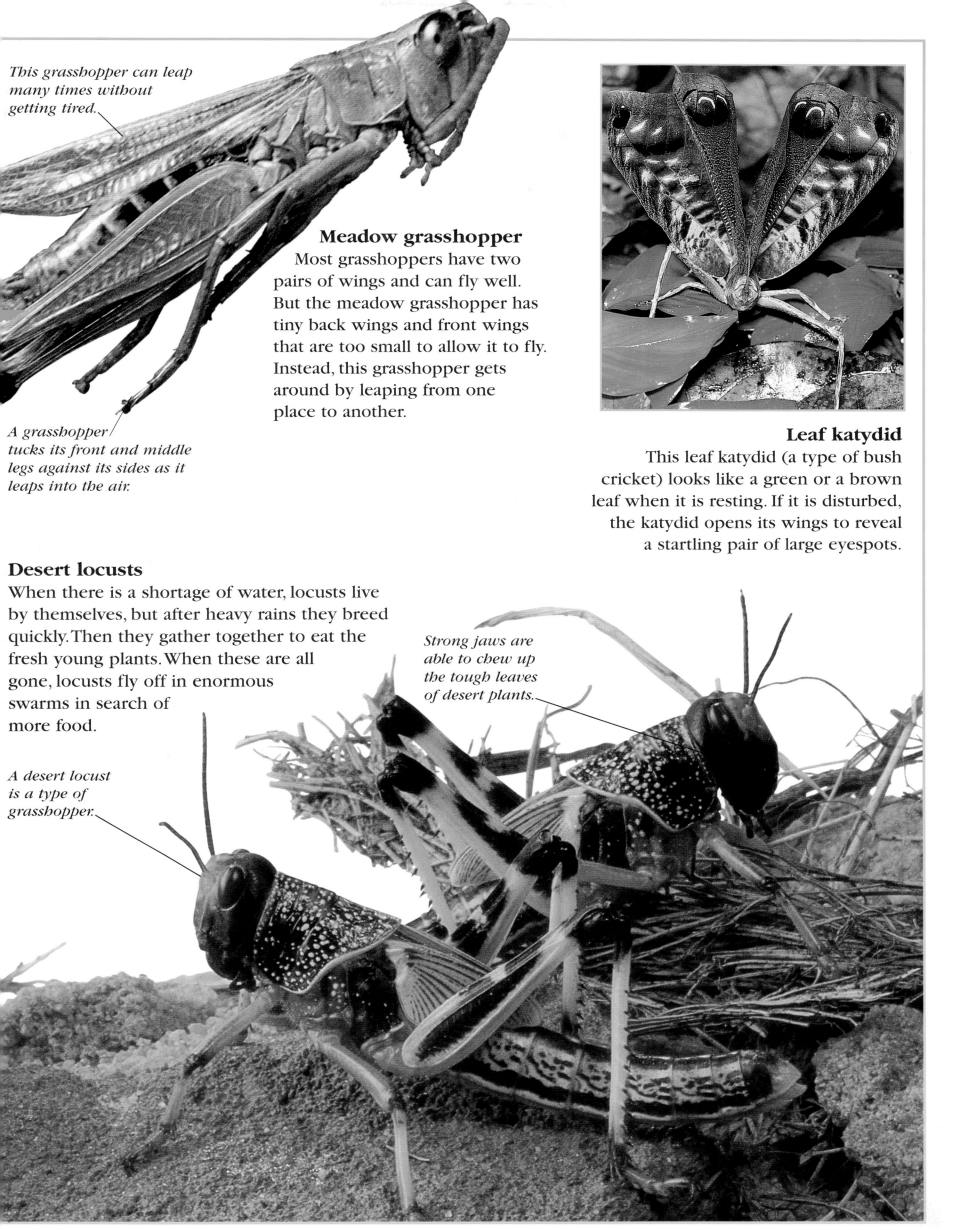

This grasshopper can leap many times without getting tired.

Meadow grasshopper

Most grasshoppers have two pairs of wings and can fly well. But the meadow grasshopper has tiny back wings and front wings that are too small to allow it to fly. Instead, this grasshopper gets around by leaping from one place to another.

A grasshopper tucks its front and middle legs against its sides as it leaps into the air.

Leaf katydid

This leaf katydid (a type of bush cricket) looks like a green or a brown leaf when it is resting. If it is disturbed, the katydid opens its wings to reveal a startling pair of large eyespots.

Desert locusts

When there is a shortage of water, locusts live by themselves, but after heavy rains they breed quickly. Then they gather together to eat the fresh young plants. When these are all gone, locusts fly off in enormous swarms in search of more food.

Strong jaws are able to chew up the tough leaves of desert plants.

A desert locust is a type of grasshopper.

Centipedes and Millipedes

Long, wriggly centipedes and millipedes have plenty of legs. But while some centipedes do live up to their name, which means "one hundred feet," there are no millipedes that have one thousand feet, as their name suggests. Centipedes hunt for small insects, worms, and grubs. Millipedes feed on dead leaves, rotting wood, and sometimes on living plants.

Burrowing centipede
This long, thin centipede burrows in the soil of woodlands and gardens. It is blind and uses its antennae to search for food by means of smell and touch. When this centipede is disturbed, it produces a bright glow to startle hungry predators.

Giant tiger centipede
The first pair of a centipede's many legs are sharp pincers that inject venom when they nip. These help them to kill their prey. This rain forest centipede has venom powerful enough to kill small rodents. Its orange and black stripes warn animals that it is dangerous.

This centipede has just over a hundred legs.

Each segment of a centipede's body has one pair of jointed legs.

Armored millipede

The armored millipede uses its strong, flat back to push itself under bark or through leaf litter. It has longer legs than most millipedes. This helps it to make a larger hole as it pushes itself through the soil.

Most millipedes curl around into a spiral when threatened. This helps to protect their soft underparts.

Millipedes have two pairs of legs on every segment.

Antenna

Powerful venom is injected by a nip from these stout claws.

Tropical millipede

Many tropical millipedes are brightly striped to warn predators that they have a secret weapon. This one has special pores along its side that squirt out foul-smelling slime and stinging chemicals if the millipede is attacked. Enemies, such as ants and spiders, beat a fast retreat!

Glossary

Abdomen
The back part of an insect's body that contains its gut and other organs.

Antennae
Two thin, long or short feelers on an insect's head. They can pick up scents from the air and are used for touching.

Camouflage
Colors and patterns on an insect that makes it look like its background. This helps an insect hide from its enemies.

Colony
A group of the same insects, such as ants, that live and work together.

Compound eyes
Eyes that are made up of thousands of tiny lenses packed closely together.

Eyespot
A pattern on an insect's wings that looks just like a big eye. This is used to frighten enemies.

Formic acid
A stinging liquid that some ants spray from the tips of their abdomen.

Hive
A place in which bees live in colonies and store honey.

Larva
The young stage of an insect's life – for example, a caterpillar.

Molt
A process in which an insect sheds its skin.

Nectar
The sweet, sugary liquid that is produced at the base of a flower's petals to attract insects.

Nymph
A young insect. Unlike a larva, a nymph looks like its parents when it hatches, but it can only fly after the final molt.

Pollen
Dusty powder that contains the male sex cells. This is used by some insects as a source of food.

Pollinate
The process through which insects transfer pollen from one flower to another. This makes new seeds.

Predator
An animal that catches and eats other animals.

Prey
An animal that is caught and eaten by a predator.

Pupa
The stage in the life cycle of some insects. The larvae stop eating and change into adult insects inside a hard case called a pupa.

Territory
An area that an insect lives in and defends.

Tropical rain forest
A forest where plenty of rain falls all year round and where the temperature is always warm.

Venom
A liquid containing harmful chemicals that one animal injects into another by means of fangs, stingers, hairs, or claws.

Index